W9-BFF-952

-FOODS OF-
BRAZIL

by Christine Velure Roholt

BELLWETHER MEDIA • MINNEAPOLIS, MN

Library of Congress Cataloging-in-Publication Data

VeLure Roholt, Christine, author.
 Foods of Brazil / by Christine VeLure Roholt.
    pages cm. -- (Express. Cook with Me)
 Summary: "Information accompanies step-by-step instructions on how to cook Brazilian food. The
text level and subject matter are intended for students in grades 3 through 7"-- Provided by publisher.
 Audience: Age 7-12.
 Audience: Grades 3-7.
 Includes bibliographical references and index.
 ISBN 978-1-62617-115-2 (hardcover : alk. paper)
 1. Cooking, Brazilian--Juvenile literature. 2. Food habits--Brazil--Juvenile literature. 3. Brazil--Social life
and customs--Juvenile literature. I. Title.
 TX716.B6V45 2014
 641.5981--dc23
                                     2014010167

This edition first published in 2015 by Bellwether Media, Inc.

Printed in the United States of America, North Mankato, MN.

Table of Contents

Cooking the Brazilian Way

Brazilian **cuisine** has been influenced by many different cultures. In the 16th century, Portuguese explorers landed in the area that would become Brazil. They found **native** peoples who had special ways of preparing local plants and animals. The **colonists** embraced much of this culture. They mixed the Amazonian cooking styles and ingredients with some of their own recipes from Portugal. Later, African **slaves** brought their own flavors to Brazilian kitchens. As Brazil welcomed more **immigrants**, other cultures added special touches to the local dishes.

Most Brazilian chefs use ingredients native to their region of the country. In the **rain forest**, this often means fresh fish from the Amazon River and a variety of **tropical** fruits. In the southern grasslands, meat from livestock is more common. Throughout the country, **cassava** forms the basis of many dishes. Rice and beans also accompany most meals.

cassava

Eating the Brazilian Way

Brazilian people eat their biggest meal at midday. They enjoy spending mealtime with friends and family, and they stay to chat even after the food is finished. A normal lunch can last one or two hours. Dinner is lighter and usually eaten with family. If Brazilian people need a snack, they stop at a street cart. Instead of taking it to go, they wait to leave until they finish eating it. They never eat or drink while walking.

Brazilian people have excellent table manners. They never speak with food in their mouths or belch at the table. They also consider it impolite to eat with their hands. They use silverware to eat almost everything, including pizza and hamburgers. If they must pick something up, they use napkins instead of bare hands.

A Melting Pot

The national dish of Brazil is *feijoada*. This stew usually includes beans, beef, and pork. Each region adds local ingredients to the stew, making feijoada as varied as Brazil's cuisine.

Regional Foods

Many of Brazil's most famous dishes can be found anywhere in the country. However, Brazil is a large country with five regions distinct in both culture and landscape. These differences inspire recipes specific to each region. Unique dishes such as these add flavor to the rich Brazilian cuisine.

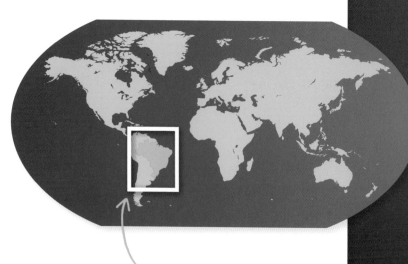

Where is Brazil?

North

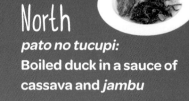

pato no tucupi:
Boiled duck in a sauce of
cassava and *jambu*

Northeast

bobó de camarão:
Shrimp stewed in a mixture
of pureed cassava, coconut
milk, and red palm oil

Central

doce abóbora:
Pumpkins or squash
stewed in sweet syrup

Southeast

cuscuz paulista:
A mixture of vegetables,
meats, and cornmeal
molded in a cake pan

South

churrasco:
Marinated and
barbecued meat

N
W — E
S

9

Coffee and Desserts

Coffee is an important part of the Brazilian day. Brazilian people usually enjoy it sweetened and very strong. Small *cafezhinos* are sipped throughout the day and also typically follow each meal. Many restaurants even include coffee for free. To cool off, Brazilian people drink fresh fruit juices. They also enjoy *agua de coco*, or coconut water. They cut the top off of an unripe coconut and sip the juice out with a straw.

Highly Caffeinated

Brazil grows and produces about one-third of all the coffee in the world.

passion fruit cheesecake

brigadeiros

Brigadeiros are the most famous Brazilian dessert. These small chocolate balls are made with sweetened condensed milk and topped with chocolate sprinkles. They are popular at birthday parties. Brazilian people also use fruit in their desserts. Passion fruit is a favorite. It flavors pies, **mousses**, and cakes. Avocados also make appearances in some Brazilian desserts.

Getting Ready to Cook

Before you begin cooking, read these safety reminders. Make sure you also read the recipes you will follow. You will want to gather all the ingredients and cooking tools right away.

Safety Reminders

 Ask an adult for permission to start cooking. An adult should be near when you use kitchen appliances or a sharp knife.

 Wash your hands with soapy water before you start cooking. Wash your hands again if you lick your fingers or handle raw meat.

 If you have long hair, tie it back. Remove any bracelets or rings that you have on.

 Wear an apron when you cook. It will protect food from dirt and your clothes from spills and splatters.

 Always use oven mitts when handling hot cookware. If you accidentally burn yourself, run the burned area under cold water and tell an adult.

 If a fire starts, call an adult immediately. Never throw water on a fire. Baking soda can smother small flames. A lid can put out a fire in a pot or pan. If flames are large and leaping, call 911 and leave the house.

 Clean up the kitchen when you are done cooking. Make sure all appliances are turned off.

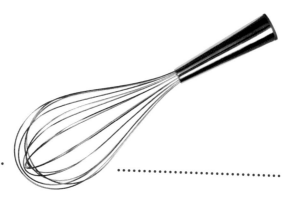

Pão de Queijo

powh jeh KAY-zho

Brazilian Cheese Rolls
Makes 24

Pão de queijo is a favorite breakfast food in much of Brazil. It is also often served as a snack with coffee or tea.

What You'll Need

- 1 cup milk
- 1/2 cup vegetable oil
- 1 teaspoon salt
- 2 cups sour cassava flour (substitute: tapioca flour)
- 2 eggs
- 1 cup grated Parmesan cheese

- saucepan
- whisk
- large bowl
- small bowl
- ice cream scooper (substitute: spoon)
- baking sheet

1

In a saucepan, combine the milk, vegetable oil, and salt. Then preheat the oven to 375 degrees Fahrenheit.

2

Use a whisk to mix the ingredients. Place over medium heat until the mixture bubbles.

3

Mix in the flour. Stir well, then let the dough cool. Transfer the dough to a large bowl.

4

Whisk the eggs in a small bowl. Add the eggs and cheese to the dough, then stir well.

5

Scoop the dough into balls. Place them on a baking sheet about 1 inch apart.

6

Bake for about 20–25 minutes or until golden brown on top. Serve warm.

Enjoy!

Did You Know?

Pão de queijo is Portuguese for "cheese bread."

Moqueca
moe-KAY-ka

Brazilian Fish Stew
Serves 4

Moqueca is traditionally cooked and served in a large clay pot. It was first made in northeastern Brazil, but there are now many kinds of moqueca enjoyed all over the country.

What You'll Need

- 1 1/2 pounds halibut (substitute: cod)
- 1/2 pound peeled shrimp
- 1/4 cup lime juice
- 4 minced garlic cloves
- salt and pepper
- 1/4 cup palm oil (substitute: olive oil)
- 1 small diced onion
- 1/4 cup diced smoked red pepper
- 2-3 diced plum tomatoes
- 1 cup coconut milk

- 1 cup vegetable stock (substitute: fish stock)
- 1/4 cup chopped cilantro
- 2 cups water (optional)
- 1 cup white rice (optional)
- large bowl
- tongs
- large saucepan
- stirring spoon
- measuring cup
- strainer
- small pot (optional)

Let's Make It!

1

In a large bowl, cover the fish and shrimp with the lime juice. Add 2 minced garlic cloves and a pinch of salt and pepper.

2

Add the oil and diced onion to a large saucepan. Sauté over medium heat for 5-7 minutes or until soft.

3

Add 2 minced garlic cloves and the diced red pepper. Cook for about 3 minutes.

4

Stir in the diced tomatoes and cook for 5 minutes.

5

Mix in the vegetable stock and coconut milk. Warm the stew, but be careful not to bring to a boil.

6

Drain the juices from the fish and shrimp. Add to the stew and cook for about 10 minutes or until the fish and shrimp are firm and white.

Enjoy!

Sprinkle cilantro over the stew and serve warm on a plate or in a bowl.

Serve with Rice

People often enjoy moqueca served with rice. To serve rice with your stew, follow these steps:

1. Bring 2 cups of water to a boil in a small pot.
2. Add the rice and cover the pot. Reduce to low heat.
3. Cook for about 20 minutes or until rice is firm and soft.

Salpicão

sal-pee-COW

Brazilian Chicken Salad
Serves 4

Salpicão is a popular salad eaten throughout Brazil. It is often served as a sandwich, wrap, or as a side dish.

What You'll Need

- 2 cooked and shredded chicken breasts
- 2 grated carrots
- 1/2 cup cooked corn
- 1/2 cup cooked peas
- 1 diced green apple
- 1 diced red apple
- 1/2 cup raisins
- 1 chopped onion
- 4 ounces shoestring potatoes

- 3/4 cup mayonnaise
- 3/4 cup crème fraiche (substitute: sour cream)
- salt and pepper
- bread (substitute: croissants)
- lettuce leaves (optional)
- large bowl
- stirring spoon

Let's Make It!

1

In a large bowl, combine the chicken, carrots, corn, and peas. Then mix in the apples, raisins, and onion.

2

Stir in 2 ounces of the shoestring potatoes.

3

Add the mayonnaise and crème fraiche, then stir well.

4

Add salt and pepper to taste.

5

If you like, place the salad on top of large lettuce leaves.

Enjoy!

Sprinkle 2 ounces of shoestring potatoes on top of the salad and serve with croissants.

Rabanada

ha-ba-NAH-da

Brazilian French Toast
Serves 4

Though *rabanadas* are similar to French toast, Brazilians do not eat them for breakfast. Instead, these desserts are traditionally enjoyed around Christmastime.

What You'll Need

- 1 baguette
- 3 eggs
- 3/8 cup milk
- 3/4 cup condensed milk
- 1/2 teaspoon vanilla extract
- 1/4 teaspoon salt
- vegetable oil
- 1/2 cup sugar
- 1 teaspoon cinnamon
- 1 tablespoon unsweetened cocoa powder

- knife
- large bowl
- whisk
- large baking dish
- tongs
- plastic wrap
- large frying pan
- fork
- paper towel

Let's Make It!

1

Cut the baguette into slices 1 inch thick.

2

Combine the eggs, milk, condensed milk, vanilla extract, and salt in a large bowl. Use a whisk to mix well.

3

Pour the mixture into a large baking dish.

4

Place the baguette slices in the baking dish. Use tongs to flip the slices so both sides are covered with the mixture.

5

Cover the dish with plastic wrap. Place in the refrigerator for at least 20 minutes.

6

Pour vegetable oil in a large frying pan over medium-high heat.

7

Use a fork to lift the baguette slices out of the dish. Let the extra mixture drip off, then place the bread in the frying pan.

8

Fry the bread for about 5 minutes. Flip the slices over and fry until golden brown.

Enjoy!

Transfer the bread to a paper towel. Mix the sugar, cinnamon, and cocoa powder, then sprinkle on the toast.

21

Glossary

cassava—a tropical plant with starchy, edible roots; cassava is also called manioc.

colonists—people who settle new land for their home country

cuisine—a style of cooking unique to a certain area or group of people

immigrants—people who leave one country to live in another country

mousses—cold, sweet foods made with whipped cream or egg whites

native—originally from a specific place

rain forest—a thick, green forest that receives a lot of rain

slaves—people who are considered property

tropical—part of the tropics; the tropics is a hot, rainy region near the equator.

To Learn More

AT THE LIBRARY

Behnke, Alison. *Cooking the Brazilian Way: Culturally Authentic Foods Including Low-Fat and Vegetarian Recipes.* Minneapolis, Minn.: Lerner Publications Company, 2004.

Locricchio, Matthew. *The Cooking of Brazil.* New York, N.Y.: Marshall Cavendish Benchmark, 2012.

Sexton, Colleen. *Brazil.* Minneapolis, Minn.: Bellwether Media, 2011.

ON THE WEB

Learning more about Brazil is as easy as 1, 2, 3.

1. Go to www.factsurfer.com.

2. Enter "Brazil" into the search box.

3. Click the "Surf" button and you will see a list of related web sites.

With factsurfer.com, finding more information is just a click away.

Index

The images in this book are reproduced through the courtesy of: HLPhoto, front cover, credits page; Gayvoronskaya_Yana, title page; Jiang Hongyan, table of contents; diogoppr, pp. 4, 9 (bottom right); Kim Nguyen, pp. 5, 19 (top center), 21; Kim Carson/ Getty Images, p. 6; Alina Solovyova-Vincent/ Getty Images, p. 7; Ifcastro/ Canstock Photo, p. 9 (top left); Paul_Brighton, p. 9 (top right); Carla Nichiata, p. 9 (middle right); Matteo Torri/ age fotostock, p. 9 (bottom right); AGorohov, pp. 10, 13; Ildi Papp, p. 11 (left); Filipe Frazao, p. 11 (right); DircinhaSW/ Getty Images, p. 12 (left); Gogo Images/ Glow Images, p. 12 (right); Beto Chagas, p. 15; Sabphoto, p. 19 (bottom center); Hong Vo, p. 19 (bottom); Ami Parikh, p. 21; all other photos courtesy of bswing.

DATE DUE

FOLLETT